THE STOMACH AND INTESTINES IN YOUR BODY

ROBERT Z. COHEN

Britannica®
Educational Publishing

IN ASSOCIATION WITH

ROSEN
EDUCATIONAL SERVICES

Published in 2015 by Britannica Educational Publishing (a trademark of Encyclopædia Britannica, Inc.) in association with The Rosen Publishing Group, Inc.
29 East 21st Street, New York, NY 10010

Distributed exclusively by Rosen Publishing.
To see additional Britannica Educational Publishing titles, go to rosenpublishing.com.

First Edition

Britannica Educational Publishing
J. E. Luebering: Director, Core Reference Group
Mary Rose McCudden: Editor, Britannica Student Encyclopedia

Rosen Publishing
Hope Lourie Killcoyne: Executive Editor
Christine Poolos: Editor
Nelson Sá: Art Director
Nicole Russo: Designer
Cindy Reiman: Photography Manager

Library of Congress Cataloging-in-Publication Data

Cohen, Robert Z., author.
The stomach and intestines in your body / Robert Z. Cohen.
     pages cm. — (Let's find out. The human body)
Audience: Grades 3 to 6.
Includes bibliographical references and index.
ISBN 978-1-62275-632-2 (library bound) — ISBN 978-1-62275-633-9 (pbk.) — ISBN 978-1-62275-634-6 (6-pack)
1. Digestive organs — Juvenile literature. 2. Digestion — Juvenile literature. 3. Human body — Juvenile literature. 4. Human physiology — Juvenile literature. I. Title.
QP145.C833 2015
612.3 — dc23
                                                                                                      2014017805

Manufactured in the United States of America

CONTENTS

An Energy Machine

Animals need food for energy and growth. To use the food they eat, they must change it into a form that the body can use. This process is called digestion. All of the parts of the body that help with digestion make up the digestive system.

In humans, the digestive system includes the mouth, the esophagus, the stomach, and the small and large intestines. The liver and the pancreas also

Kids need a healthy and balanced diet to provide the nutrition their body needs to grow.

help in digestion. The hardest working digestive organs are the stomach and intestines. Think of them as the machine that refines and pumps the fuel that provides us with energy.

THINK ABOUT IT

Your brain makes up less than 2 percent of your weight but uses up almost 20 percent of all the energy you consume! How does your diet affect your brain?

Our digestive system turns food from plants and animals into the energy we need to live an active life.

THE DIGESTIVE SYSTEM

Digestion begins in the mouth. There, teeth chew food into smaller pieces. When a person swallows food it passes through the throat into the esophagus.

The esophagus is a tube that connects to the stomach. The walls of the esophagus move in waves to push the food down to

The food we eat is broken down into chemicals that our body can use.

Chyme is a thick mixture made in the stomach after chewing and stomach action has processed our food.

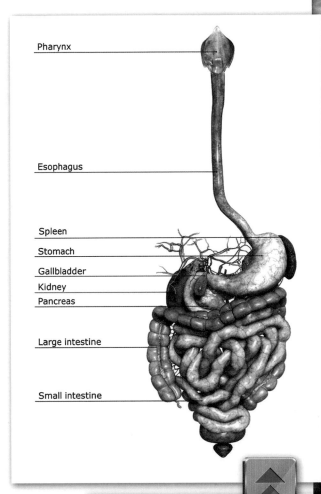

Pharynx

Esophagus

Spleen
Stomach
Gallbladder
Kidney
Pancreas

Large intestine

Small intestine

the stomach. The walls of the stomach produce substances that help break down the chewed food into chyme.

From the stomach, the chyme is pushed into the small intestine. There, digestive fluids turn the chyme into chemicals that the body can use. Leftover material enters the large intestine, which removes water and salts and creates solid waste that will pass out of the body.

Digestion begins when food moves from the mouth through the pharynx to the esophagus.

THE HUMAN STOMACH

The stomach is like a hollow sac. It can expand to accept and store food. The stomach is located in the upper left side of the belly, or abdomen. An adult's stomach is about 10 inches (25 centimeters) long. When it expands, it can hold as much as 1 quart (0.9 liter) of food.

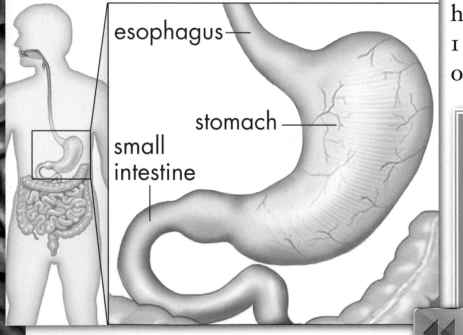

esophagus—

stomach —

small intestine

The stomach is a large, stretchy bag that is in constant motion.

Glands in the stomach produce gastric juices. These juices contain substances called enzymes and a strong chemical known as hydrochloric acid. The stomach muscles mix the food and gastric juices

Enzymes are molecules that build up or break down other molecules. In the case of digestion, they help to break down food particles.

A good meal should include fiber-rich vegetables that help the digestive process and provide needed energy.

together. The enzymes and acid in the juices work together to help soften and dissolve solid pieces of food. This process creates chyme. The stomach does not digest itself because the walls produce thick mucus that protects the stomach from the gastric acid.

At the bottom of the stomach, a muscle called the pylorus helps squeeze the chyme into the small intestine. It takes several hours for food to move through the stomach and into the small intestine. Even after the stomach has emptied, the stomach muscles continue to move. You feel this as hunger.

At meal times, the brain lets the stomach know that it is time to get to work again.

Special cells that are directly linked to the brain tell us to feel satisfied after a good meal.

THINK ABOUT IT

When your stomach "growls," it is the sound of your stomach walls mixing food and gastric juices. When do you notice your stomach making sounds?

The stomach also has many nerve cells called neurons, which send signals to the brain. When you feel good after eating food, this is a signal from your stomach's neurons.

Stomachs of Other Animals

Cows, giraffes, and deer eat grass and leaves, which are hard to digest. The stomachs of these animals have four different chambers. After food is swallowed, it is moistened in the first two chambers. It returns to the

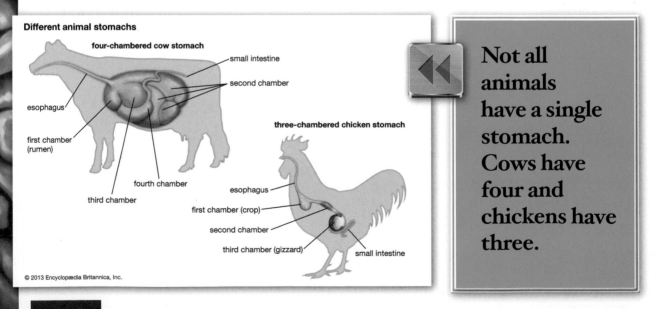

Different animal stomachs

four-chambered cow stomach

small intestine

second chamber

esophagus

first chamber (rumen)

fourth chamber

third chamber

three-chambered chicken stomach

esophagus

first chamber (crop)

second chamber

third chamber (gizzard)

small intestine

© 2013 Encyclopædia Britannica, Inc.

Not all animals have a single stomach. Cows have four and chickens have three.

animals' mouths to be chewed again as cud. Then it is swallowed again and returned to the final two stomach chambers.

Birds have three stomach chambers. Some animals have no stomach at all! Many fish, such as carp, and even mammals such as the Australian duck-billed platypus eat foods that do not require an acid-producing stomach chamber. Their food goes directly from their esophagus into their intestines.

The platypus is a truly unique creature, with a ducklike bill and powerful venom in its claws. It is the only mammal that reproduces by laying eggs.

THE SMALL INTESTINE

The real job of turning food into energy takes place in the small intestine. The small intestine can be 22 to 25 feet (6.7 to 7.6 meters) long. It is the longest part of the digestive system.

The first section of the small intestine is called the duodenum. Two large organs, the liver and the pancreas, are connected to the duodenum by ducts, or tubes. The organs send digestive juices to

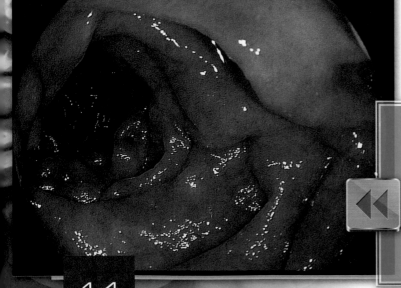

The duodenum is the beginning of the small intestine. Many chemicals and enzymes enter the digestive system here.

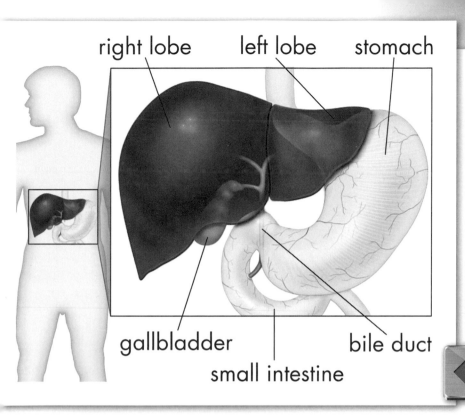

right lobe   left lobe   stomach

gallbladder   bile duct

small intestine

◀◀

The liver is one of the largest organs in the human body. It performs many important functions.

Bile is a fluid made in the liver that helps digest fats. It changes the color of food waste to brown or yellow.

the small intestine through these ducts. Juice from the pancreas helps to break down carbohydrates, proteins, and fats. The liver makes bile, which helps to break down fat. The bile is stored in the gallbladder, a small hollow organ located just under the liver. The walls of the intestine produce other juices.

All these fluids break down most of the remains of the food into simple chemicals. The chemicals enter the bloodstream through

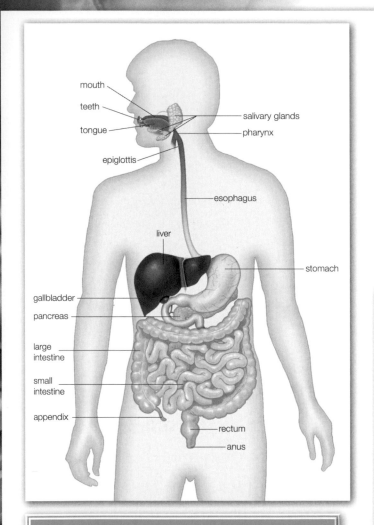

mouth
teeth
tongue
epiglottis
salivary glands
pharynx
esophagus
liver
gallbladder
pancreas
large intestine
small intestine
appendix
stomach
rectum
anus

Food travels a long and winding path, from the mouth all the way to the rectum.

THINK ABOUT IT

The walls of the small intestine have many folds. These increase the surface area inside the intestine. How does that help the body get the chemicals it needs?

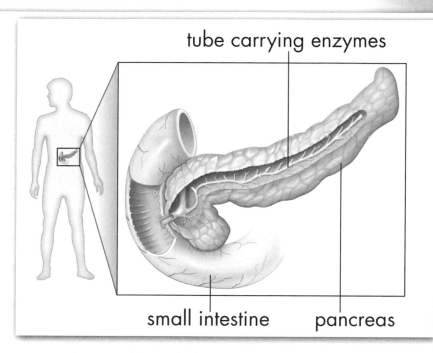

tube carrying enzymes

small intestine   pancreas

Some enzymes are responsible for speeding up the process of digestion.

the walls of the small intestine. This process takes from three to six hours. The blood carries the chemicals to the body's cells. The body then uses those chemicals as fuel for energy and growth.

The small intestine has a special kind of muscle that squeezes and relaxes in a wavelike motion. It is like the muscles in the esophagus and the stomach. The motion of the muscle pushes food and waste through the intestine.

The Large Intestine

Some substances, like plant fibers, cannot be broken down. These substances pass from the small intestine into the large intestine, or colon. The large intestine is much shorter and wider than the small intestine.

The first section of the large intestine absorbs fluids and salts. The second section removes more water. This process turns the waste material from a liquid to a solid. The last section of the colon is a holding area for waste.

The waste, called feces or stool, passes

The primary function of the large intestine is to absorb water and some minerals.

into the lower area of the large intestine called the rectum until it is expelled from the body. The work of the large intestine usually takes between one and two days.

COMPARE AND CONTRAST

High-fiber foods include cereals, salad, and beans. Low-fiber foods include meat and dairy products. How does fiber in your diet affect your digestive system?

Fiber is material that does not digest easily or at all. It is one of the most important types of food in our diets.

THE ROLE OF BACTERIA

The intestines, especially the colon, contain large numbers of bacteria. Bacteria are tiny, single-cell organisms. Some bacteria can be harmful to the body, but many, called probiotics, are necessary for good health. Bacteria help in digesting the food that moves through the intestines. They are also important because

Active, helpful bacteria are found in many foods, especially fermented foods such as yogurt.

they produce some vitamins, including vitamin K and certain B vitamins.

Bacteria in the intestines help with the body's immune system as well. They cause the solid waste in the colon to ferment, producing gas. Fermentation produces helpful chemicals that keep the lining of the intestines healthy. The lining can keep germs from passing into the body and causing an infection.

Probiotics are helpful bacteria that can be found in many fermented foods, such as yogurt or kefir.

Many of the helpful bacteria in the intestines are found in the colon.

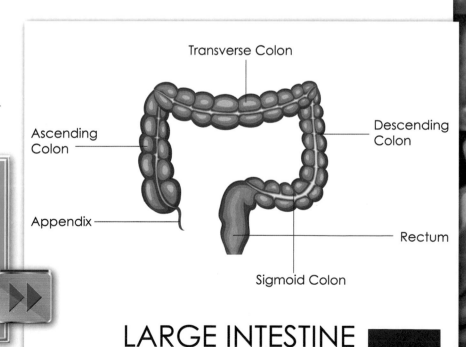

Transverse Colon

Ascending Colon

Appendix

Descending Colon

Rectum

Sigmoid Colon

LARGE INTESTINE

THE RECTUM

The rectum is at the end of the large intestine. The stool that is left at the end of the digestive process is stored there. As stool fills the rectum, the walls of the rectum expand. The walls contain special nerves that tell the brain when to push the waste out. That is when we feel that it is time to visit the bathroom.

Sometimes the feces become dry and hard and do not pass easily through the colon. This is called constipation. Diarrhea happens

The rectum is the final destination before food is expelled as waste material.

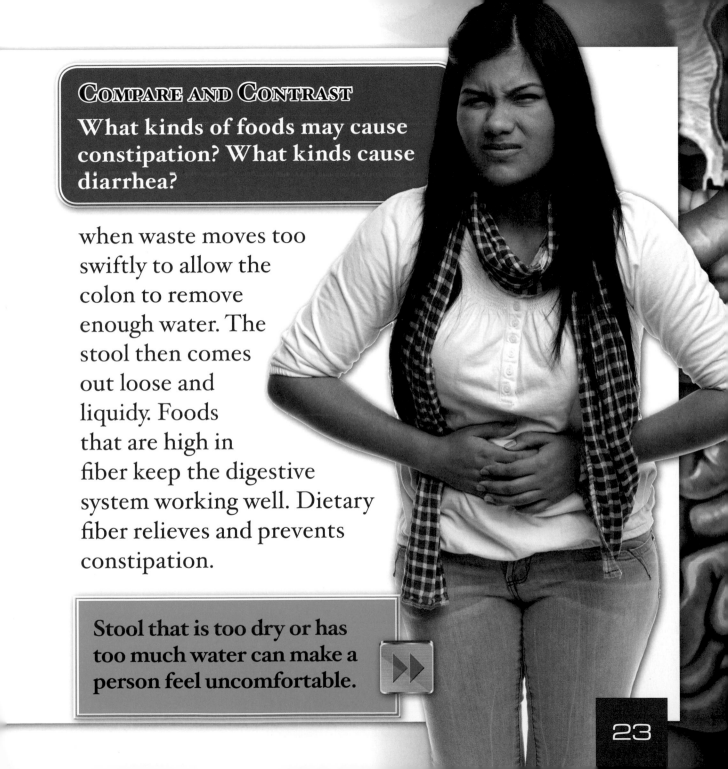

COMPARE AND CONTRAST

What kinds of foods may cause constipation? What kinds cause diarrhea?

when waste moves too swiftly to allow the colon to remove enough water. The stool then comes out loose and liquidy. Foods that are high in fiber keep the digestive system working well. Dietary fiber relieves and prevents constipation.

Stool that is too dry or has too much water can make a person feel uncomfortable.

PROBLEMS WITH DIGESTION

Many stomach or intestinal pains are not very serious. A pain in your belly might just mean that you ate too much or ate too fast. Greasy or spicy food can also cause a stomachache.

One kind of pain that is more serious is appendicitis, which is a swelling of the appendix. The appendix is a finger-sized tube attached to the large intestine

Too much greasy food, like cheeseburgers, can give you a bellyache.

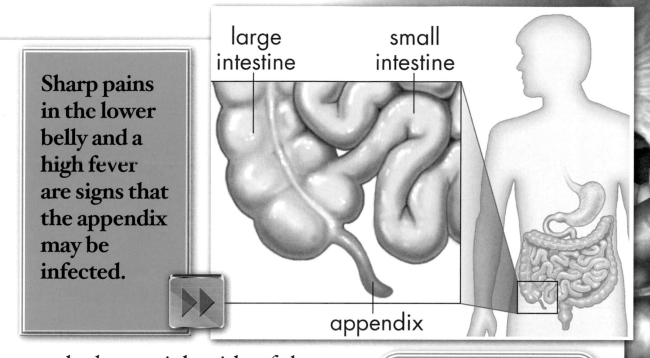

large intestine

small intestine

appendix

Sharp pains in the lower belly and a high fever are signs that the appendix may be infected.

on the lower right side of the abdomen. If a bit of digestive waste blocks the opening of the appendix, the appendix can become painful and infected. If the swelling continues, the appendix can burst, which can be very dangerous. Doctors treat appendicitis by removing the appendix.

Appendicitis is swelling and infection of the appendix.

Other digestive problems include conditions called heartburn and acid reflux. These happen when

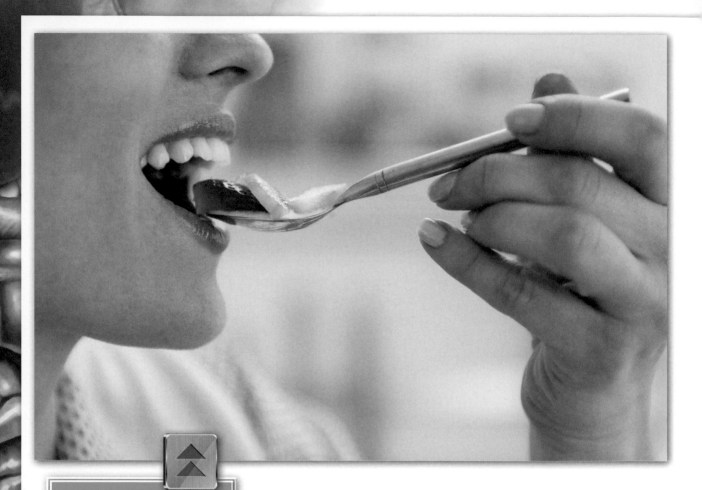

Doctors suggest eating healthy foods to avoid stomach problems.

food particles back up into the esophagus from the stomach. These problems can be treated with medicines and changes to a person's diet.

Think About It

Think about the role your intestines play in your body. Why do you think a blockage in the intestines can be so dangerous?

Sores called ulcers are problems in the stomach. Sometimes the mucus lining the stomach cannot keep the stomach acid from eating away at the lining. Ulcers can develop as a result.

It can be very dangerous if the intestines become blocked. A doctor may have to perform surgery to remove the blockage. One thing that can block the intestines is a tumor.

A healthy digestive system is important for people who want to live active lives.

Healthy Digestion

Your stomach and intestines work all day, every day, without a rest for your entire life. Keeping your digestive system healthy is as easy as paying attention to how you eat. Taking time while you eat

Your stomach and intestines will be with you for life, so it is important to take good care of them.

and chewing your food well are the first steps to good digestion.

It is also important to eat a mix of healthy foods containing fiber like cereals, grains, and fresh fruit and vegetables. Eating fermented foods such as yogurt and natural pickles aids helpful bacteria to do their job in your intestines. Learn more about what foods provide the best sources of energy and what foods to avoid.

COMPARE AND CONTRAST

People who eat lots of fast foods often gain weight and have little energy. What foods can fill you up and give you energy, without weight gain?

Learning good eating habits now will mean a healthier and happier belly in the future.

GLOSSARY

appendix A finger-sized tube attached to the large intestine.

bacteria Tiny organisms made of single cells.

carbohydrate A kind of nutrient that gives the body most of the energy it needs.

cell The tiny unit that is the basic building block of living things.

colon The middle part of the large intestine; sometimes used for the whole large intestine.

constipation Abnormally difficult or infrequent bowel movements.

diarrhea Abnormally frequent and watery bowel movements.

digestion The process by which food is broken down into simpler forms in the body.

duodenum The first part of the small intestine.

enzyme A complex protein that speeds up actions of other cells.

fermentation A chemical change that is brought about by tiny organisms such as yeasts, bacteria, and molds.

fiber Indigestible food material.

gland Tissues in the body that produce substances that help other tissues or organs function properly.

liver A large organ that produces bile and cleans blood.

molecule The smallest particle of a substance having all the characteristics of that substance.

mucus A slippery, moist substance that protects body membranes.

neuron A cell that is the basic unit of the nervous system.

pancreas A large gland that produces digestive enzymes and insulin.

protein A nutrient that is needed for body tissue to grow and repair itself.

rectum The end of the large intestine.

For More Information

Books

Burstein, John. *The Dynamic Digestive System: How Does My Stomach Work?* New York, NY: Crabtree Publishing Company, 2009.

Cobb, Vicky. *Your Body Battles a Stomachache*. Minneapolis, MN: Lerner Publishing Group, 2009.

Donovan, Sandy. *Rumble and Spew: Gross Stuff in Your Stomach and Intestines*. Minneapolis, MN: Lerner Publishing Group, 2010.

Halvorson, Karin. *Inside the Stomach*. Minneapolis, MN: ABDO Publishing, 2013.

Manley, Heather. *The Lucky Escape: An Imaginative Journey Through the Digestive System*. Amazon Digital Services, Inc., 2013.

Taylor-Butler, Christine. *The Digestive System*. New York, NY: Scholastic Books, 2008.

Websites

Because of the changing nature of Internet links, Rosen Publishing has developed an online list of websites related to the subject of this book. This site is updated regularly. Please use this link to access this list:

http://www.rosenlinks.com/LFO/Stom

Index